Easy Piano

Disney's
My First Song Book
Volume 3
A TREASURY OF FAVORITE SONGS TO SING AND PLAY

The following songs are the property of:
Bourne Co.
Music Publishers
5 West 37th Street
New York, NY 10018

Baby Mine
Give a Little Whistle
Heigh-Ho
I'm Wishing
I've Got No Strings
Some Day My Prince Will Come
When I See an Elephant Fly
When You Wish Upon a Star
Whistle While You Work
Who's Afraid of the Big Bad Wolf?

ISBN 978-1-4234-5629-2

Walt Disney Music Company
Wonderland Music Company, Inc.

DISTRIBUTED BY

7777 W. BLUEMOUND RD. P.O. BOX 13819 MILWAUKEE, WI 53213

Visit Hal Leonard Online at
www.halleonard.com

Contents

5   Alice in Wonderland

9   The Unbirthday Song
Alice in Wonderland

13   Little April Shower
Bambi

20   Baby Mine

17   When I See an Elephant Fly
Dumbo

25   A Spoonful of Sugar
Mary Poppins

28   Mickey Mouse March
The Mickey Mouse Club

31 Never Smile at a Crocodile
Peter Pan

35 Give a Little Whistle
38 I've Got No Strings
41 When You Wish Upon a Star
Pinocchio

45 Heigh-Ho
48 I'm Wishing
52 Some Day My Prince Will Come
55 Whistle While You Work
Snow White and the Seven Dwarfs

59 Who's Afraid of the Big Bad Wolf?
Three Little Pigs

Alice in Wonderland

from Walt Disney's *Alice in Wonderland*

Words by Bob Hilliard • Music by Sammy Fain

Moderately

Al - ice in Won - der - land, how do you get to Won - der - land? O - ver the hill or un - der - land or just be - hind the tree?

Gm F Gm7 C7

When clouds go roll - ing by, they roll a - way and

F Gm7 C7 F Dm Bm7 E7

leave the sky. Where is the land be - yond the eye that peo - ple can - not

Am D7 Gm7 C7 F Gm7/C C7

see?_____ Where can it be? Where do

F/C Gm7/C C7 F/C F Dm6 E7♭9

stars go? Where is the cres - cent moon? They must be

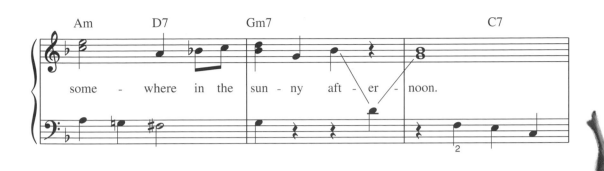

some - where in the sun - ny aft - er - noon.

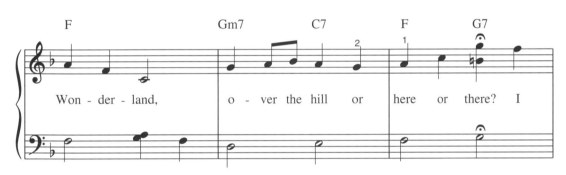

Al - ice in Won - der - land, where is the path to

Won - der - land, o - ver the hill or here or there? I

Gm7/C   C7

1.
F

2.
F   Fmaj7

won - der   where.   where.
rit.

The Unbirthday Song

from Walt Disney's *Alice in Wonderland*

Words and Music by Mack David, Al Hoffman and Jerry Livingston

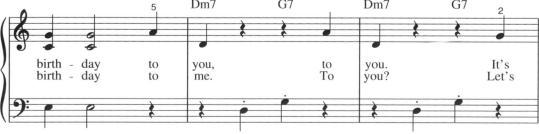

C　　　　　　　　　Dm7　　G7　　　Dm　　　A7

great　　to drink　to　　some - one　and　I　　guess that　you　will
all　con - grat - u -　late　me　with　a　　pres - ent,　I　a -

Dm　F#dim　G7sus　　G7　　　Dm7　G7　　　C　F#dim

do,　　a　ver - y　mer-ry un - birth - day　　to　you.
gree,　a　ver - y　mer-ry un - birth - day　　to　me.

G7　　G　　C　　　　　　　　　　　　　　　　　Opt. 8va - -

A　ver - y　mer-ry un - birth - day　　to　us,　　　to
A　ver - y　mer-ry un - birth - day　　to　all,　　　to

Opt. 8va _ _

us,　　a　ver - y　mer-ry un - birth - day　to　us,　　　to
all,　　a　ver - y　mer-ry un - birth - day　to　all,　　　to

Dm7　　G7

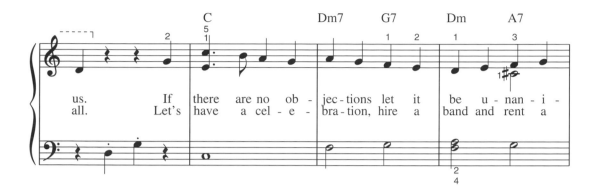

us. If there are no ob-jec-tions let it be u-nan-i-
all. Let's have a cel-e-bra-tion, hire a band and rent a

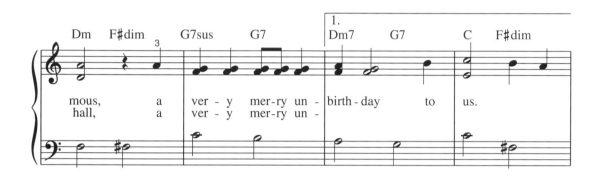

mous, a ver-y mer-ry un-birth-day to us.
hall, a ver-y mer-ry un-

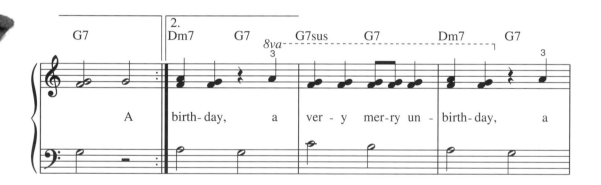

A birth-day, a ver-y mer-ry un-birth-day, a

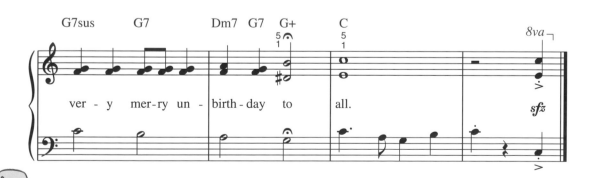

ver-y mer-ry un-birth-day to all.

Little April Shower

from Walt Disney's *Bambi*

Words by Larry Morey • Music by Frank Churchill

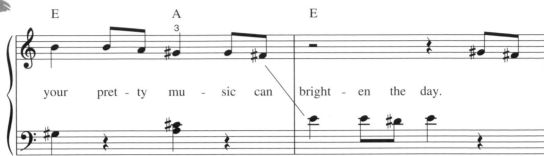

E   A   E

your pret-ty mu – sic can bright-en the day.

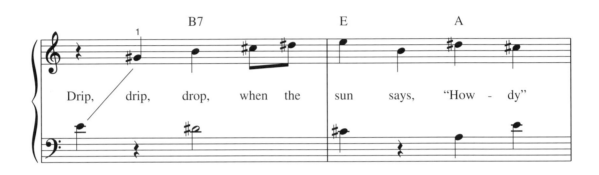

B7   E   A

Drip, drip, drop, when the sun says, "How – dy"

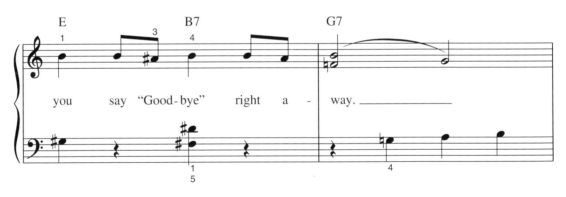

E   B7   G7

you say "Good-bye" right a – way. _____

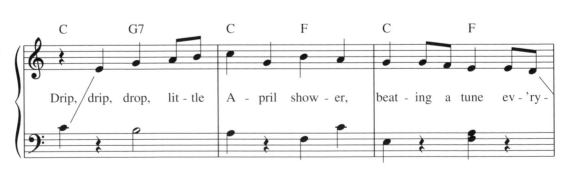

C G7   C F   C F

Drip, drip, drop, lit-tle A – pril show – er, beat-ing a tune ev-'ry-

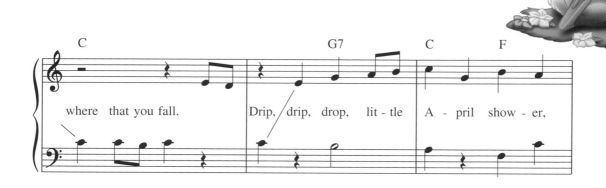

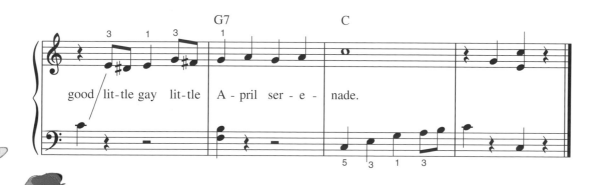

When I See an Elephant Fly

from Walt Disney's *Dumbo*

Words by Ned Washington • Music by Oliver Wallace

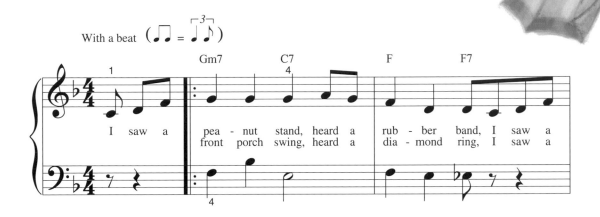

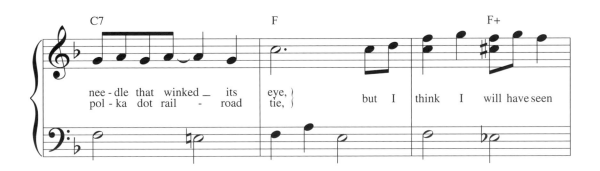

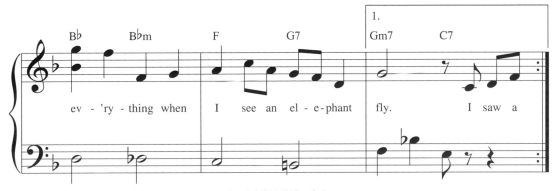

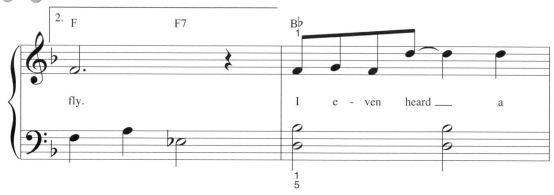

fly.   I   e - ven heard ___ a

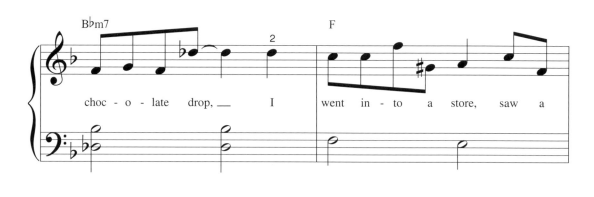

choc - o - late drop, ___ I   went in - to a store, saw a

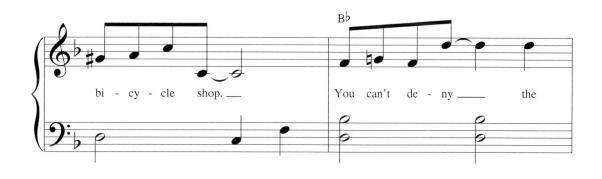

bi - cy - cle shop. ___   You can't de - ny ___   the

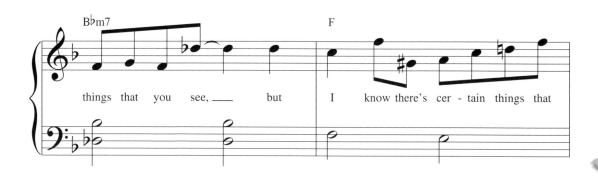

things that you see, ___ but   I   know there's cer - tain things that

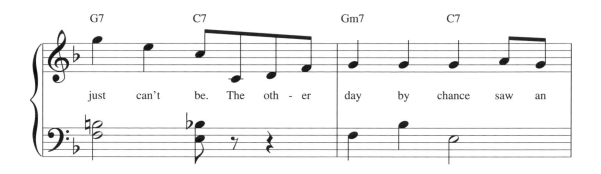

just can't be. The oth - er day by chance saw an

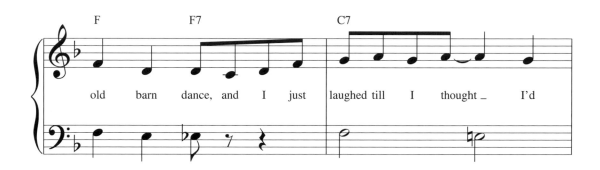

old barn dance, and I just laughed till I thought _ I'd

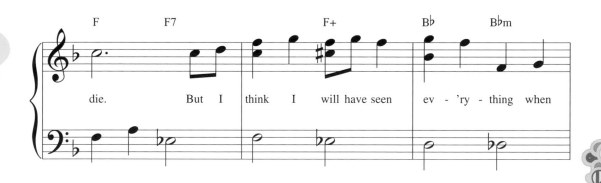

die. But I think I will have seen ev - 'ry - thing when

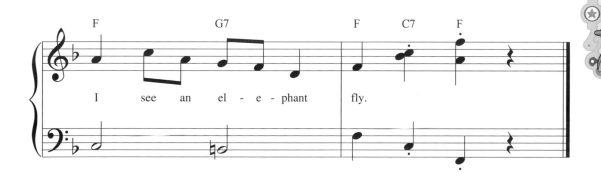

I see an el - e - phant fly.

Baby Mine

from Walt Disney's *Dumbo*

Words by Ned Washington • Music by Frank Churchill

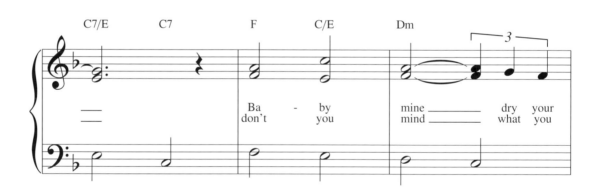

Gm7 ... Gm ... Gdim

head   close to my   heart,   nev - er to   part,   Ba - by of
eyes spar - kle and   shine,   nev - er a   tear,   Ba - by of

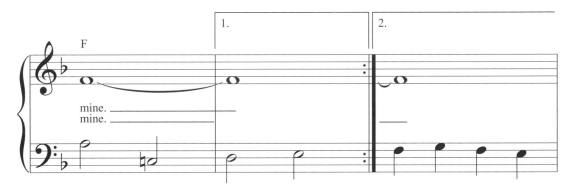

F

1.   2.

mine. _____
mine. _____

Slightly faster

Dm ... Em7

If   they   knew   sweet lit - tle   you, _____

A7 ... Dm

_____   they'd   end   up   lov - ing you,

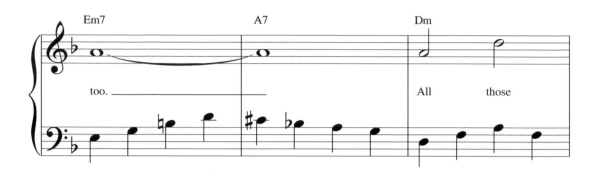

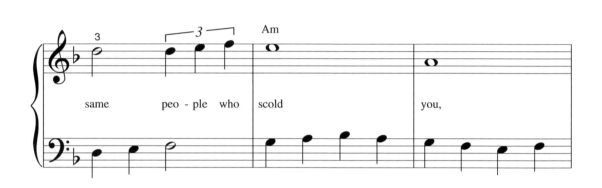

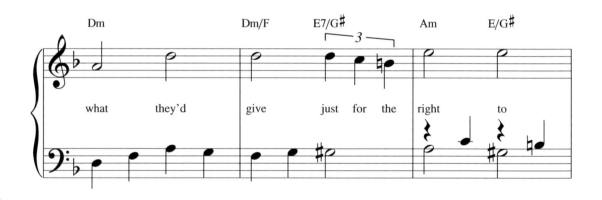

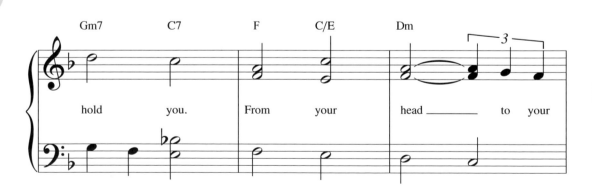

Gm7	C7/E	C7	F	C/E

toes _____ you're not

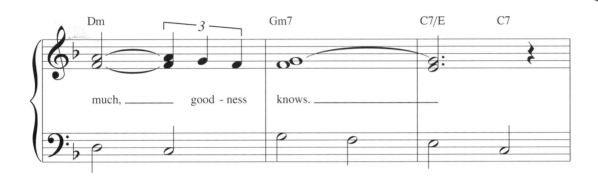

Dm	3	Gm7	C7/E	C7

much, _____ good - ness knows. _____

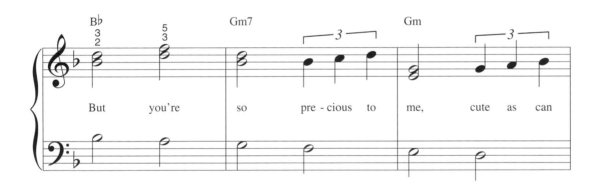

B♭	Gm7	3	Gm	3

But you're so pre - cious to me, cute as can

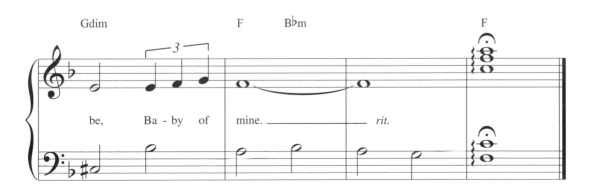

Gdim	F	B♭m	F

be, Ba - by of mine. _____ *rit.*

A Spoonful of Sugar

from Walt Disney's *Mary Poppins*

Words and Music by Richard M. Sherman and Robert B. Sherman

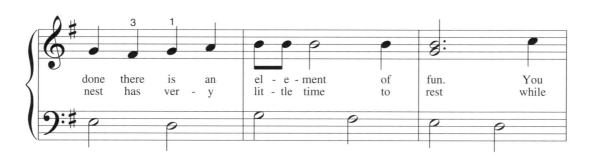

1. In ev-'ry job that must be
2. feath - er - ing his
3. *(See additional lyrics)*

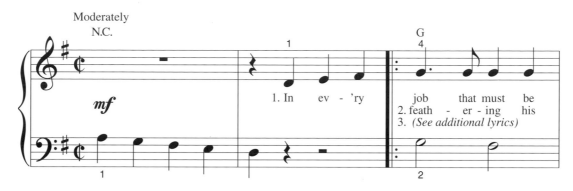

done there is an el - e - ment of fun. You
nest has ver - y lit - tle time to rest. You while

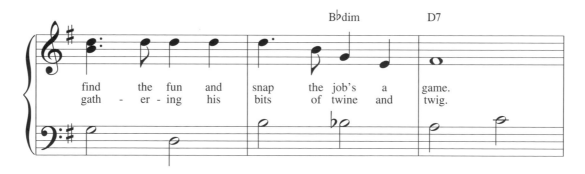

find the fun and snap the job's a game.
gath - er - ing his bits of twine and twig.

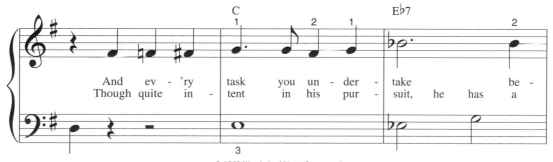

And ev - 'ry task you un - der - take be a
Though quite in - tent in his pur - suit, he has a

G   A7   D7

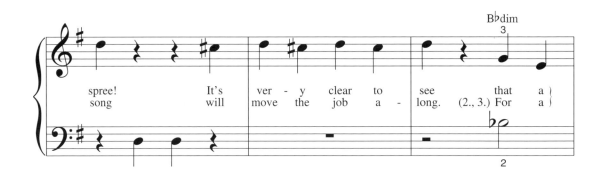

comes   a   piece   of   cake.   A   lark!   A

mer - ry tune to   toot.   He   knows   a

B♭dim

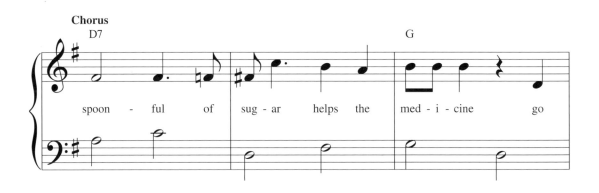

spree!   It's   ver - y   clear   to   see   that   a ⎱

song   will   move   the   job   a - long. (2., 3.) For   a ⎰

Chorus

D7   G

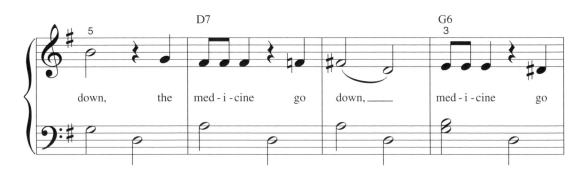

spoon - ful   of   sug - ar   helps   the   med - i - cine   go

D7   G6

down,   the   med - i - cine   go   down, ___   med - i - cine   go

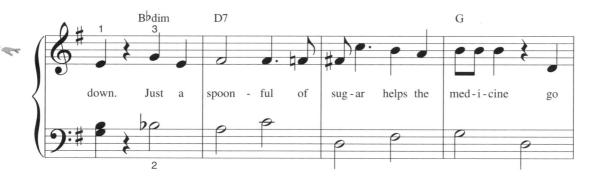

down. Just a spoon - ful of sug - ar helps the med - i - cine go

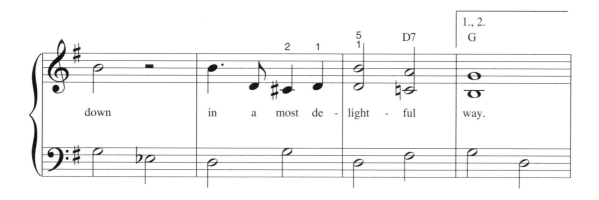

down in a most de - light - ful way.

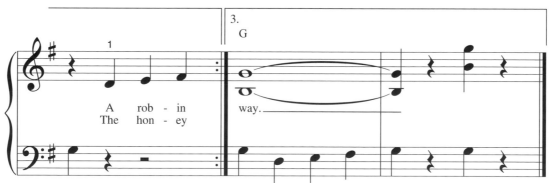

A rob - in
The hon - ey   way.

Additional Lyrics

3. The honey bees that fetch the nectar
From the flowers to the comb
Never tire of ever buzzing to and fro,
Because they take a little nip
From every flower that they sip.
And hence, they find their task is not a grind.
Chorus

MICKEY MOUSE MARCH

from Walt Disney's *The Mickey Mouse Club*

Words and Music by Jimmy Dodd

Who's the lead - er of the club that's made for you and me?
Hey, there! Hi, there! Ho, there! You're as wel - come as can be!

M - I - C - K - E - Y M - O - U - S - E!
M - I - C - K - E - Y M - O - U - S -

E! Mick - ey Mouse! _____ Mick - ey Mouse. _____
(Shout) Mick - ey Mouse! (Shout) Mick - ey

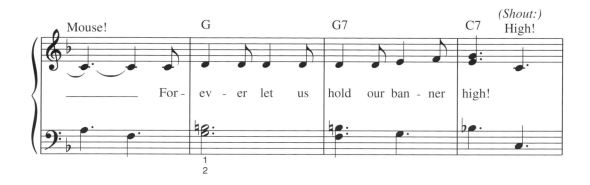

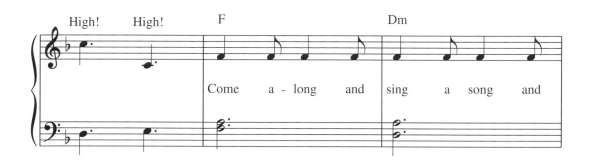

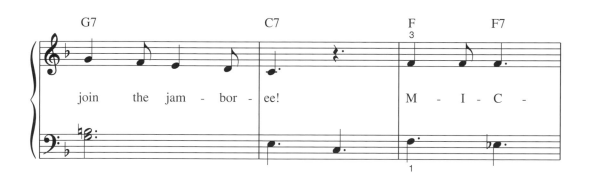

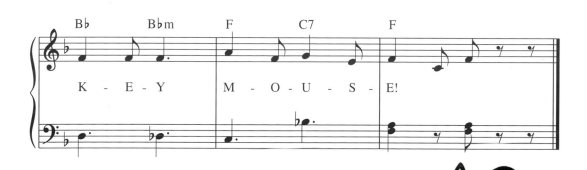

Never Smile at a Crocodile

from Walt Disney's *Peter Pan*

Words by Jack Lawrence • Music by Frank Churchill

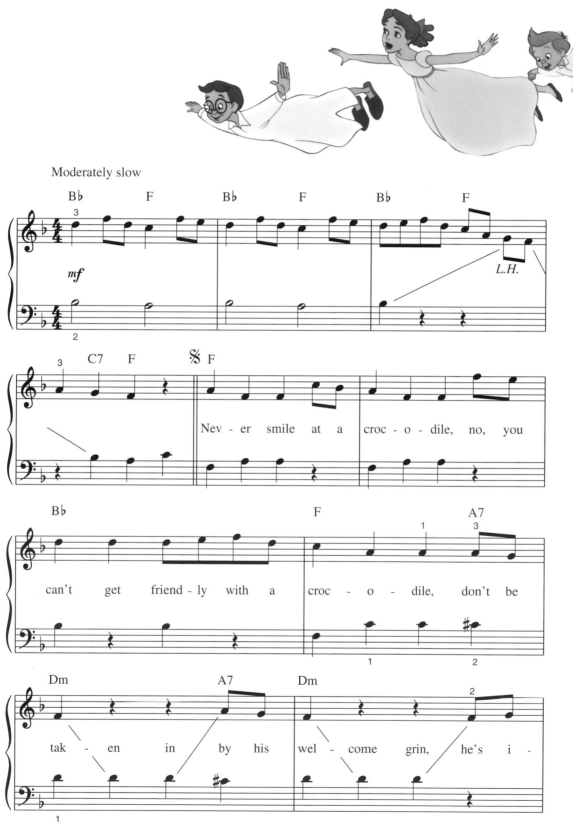

Moderately slow

Nev - er smile at a croc - o - dile, no, you can't get friend - ly with a croc - o - dile, don't be tak - en in by his wel - come grin, he's i -

mag - in - ing how well you'd fit with - in his skin.

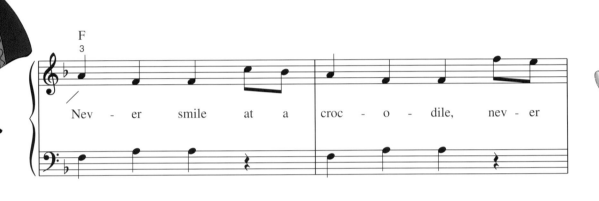

Nev - er smile at a croc - o - dile, nev - er

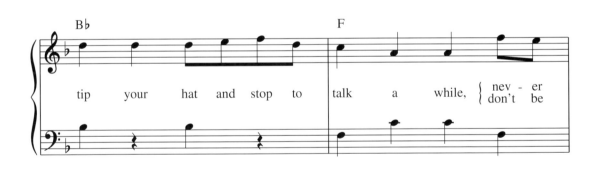

tip your hat and stop to talk a while, { nev - er
                                          don't be

run, walk a - way, say "Good - night" not "Good day!" } Clear the
rude, nev - er mock, throw a kiss, not a rock.

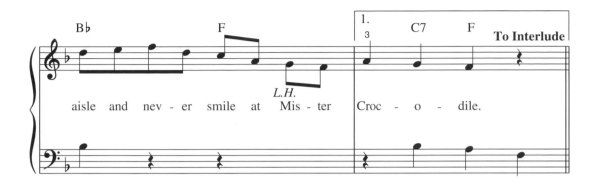

aisle and nev-er smile at Mis-ter | Croc - o - dile.

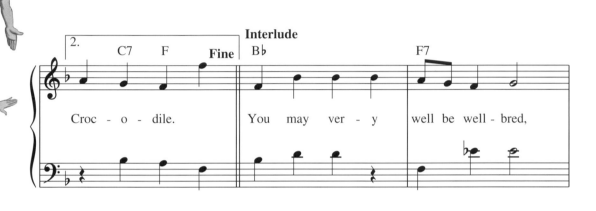

Croc - o - dile. | You may ver-y | well be well - bred,

lots of et - i - | quette in your head, | but there's al - ways

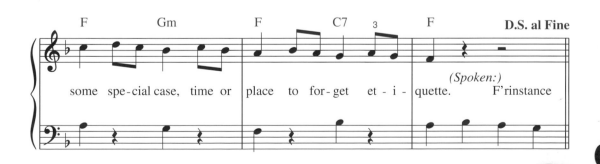

some spe-cial case, time or | place to for-get et - i - | quette. *(Spoken:)* F'rinstance

Give a Little Whistle

from Walt Disney's *Pinocchio*

Words by Ned Washington • Music by Leigh Harline

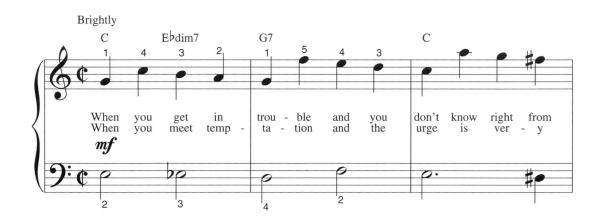

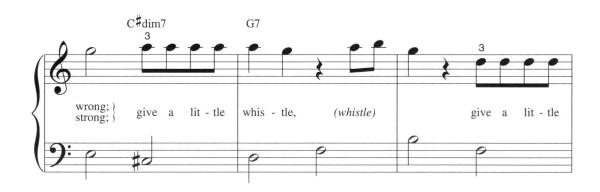

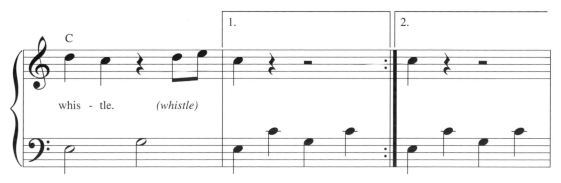

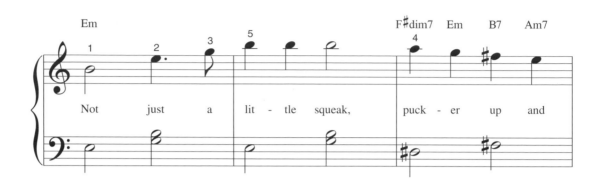

Em ... F#dim7 Em B7 Am7

Not just a lit - tle squeak, puck - er up and

B7

blow. And if your whis - tle's weak,

Em D#dim7 G7 C E♭dim7

yell, "Jim - i - ny Cric - ket." Take the straight and

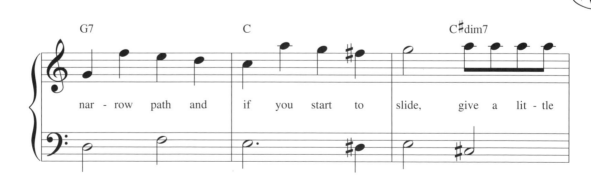

G7 C C#dim7

nar - row path and if you start to slide, give a lit - tle

whis - tle, *(whistle)* give a lit - tle whis - tle. *(whistle)*

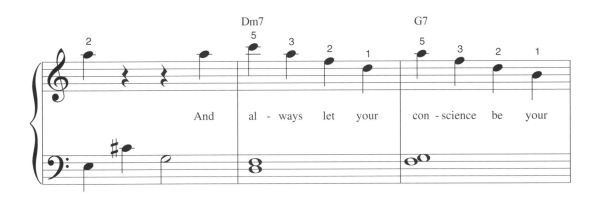

And al - ways let your con - science be your

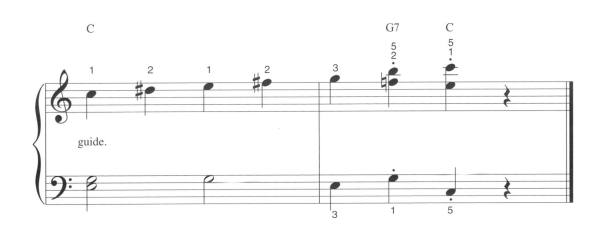

guide.

I've Got No Strings

from Walt Disney's *Pinocchio*

Words by Ned Washington • Music by Leigh Harline

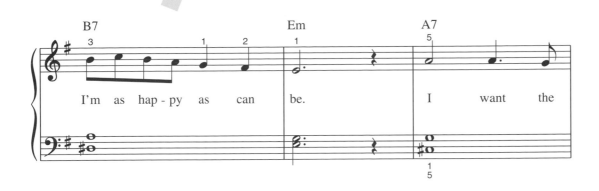

B7   Em   A7

I'm as hap - py as can   be.   I   want   the

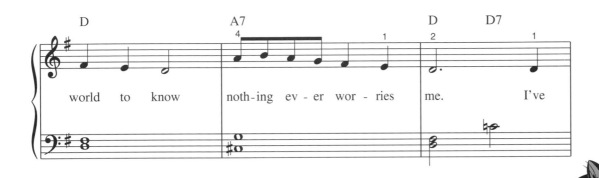

D   A7   D   D7

world to know   noth - ing ev - er wor - ries   me.   I've

G   Am7   D7   Am7   D7   G

got no strings so I have fun, I'm not tied up to an - y - one.

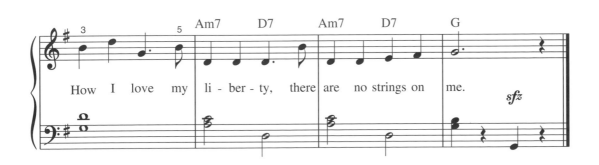

G   Am7   D7   Am7   D7   G

How I love my li - ber - ty, there are no strings on me.   sfz

When You Wish Upon a Star

from Walt Disney's *Pinocchio*

Words by Ned Washington • Music by Leigh Harline

When you wish up - on a star,
If your heart is in your dream,

makes no dif - f'rence
no re - quest is

who you are,
too ex - treme,

an - y - thing your
when you wish up -

heart de - sires will
on a star as

come to
dream - ers

you.

do. Fate is kind.

She brings to those who love

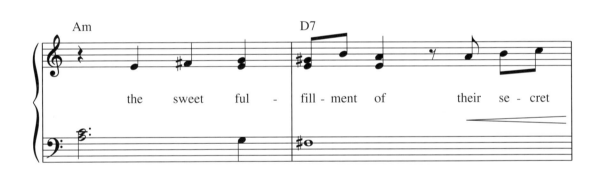

the sweet ful - fill - ment of their se - cret

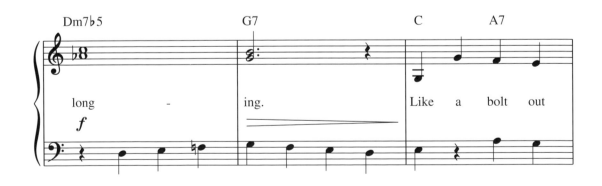

long - ing. Like a bolt out

of the blue,   fate steps in and   sees you through.

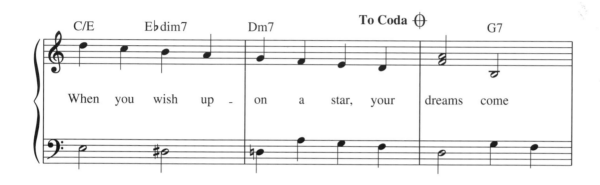

To Coda ⊕

When you wish up - on a star, your dreams come

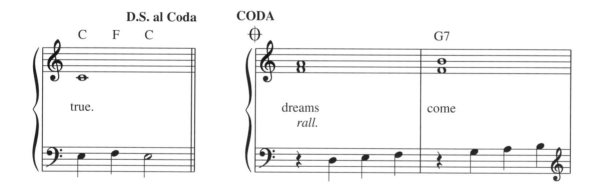

D.S. al Coda   **CODA**

true.

dreams   come
rall.

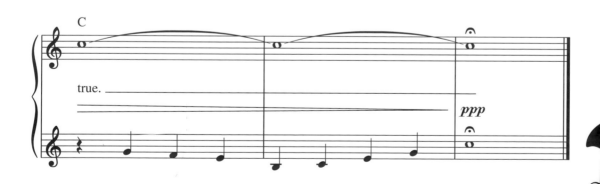

true. _____

ppp

Heigh-Ho

THE DWARFS' MARCHING SONG

from Walt Disney's *Snow White and the Seven Dwarfs*

Words by Larry Morey • Music by Frank Churchill

Em ... **Eb+**

ain't a bet-ter thing than a tune, than a tune, you can

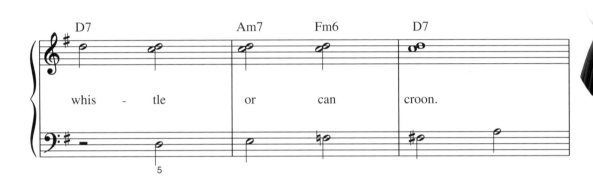

D7 ... **Am7** **Fm6** **D7**

whis - tle or can croon.

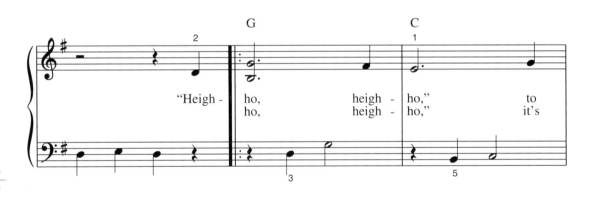

G ... **C**

"Heigh - ho, heigh - ho," to
ho, heigh - ho," it's

A7 ... **D7** ... **C** **G/B**

make your trou - bles go, just keep on sing - ing
home from work we go, *(Whistle)* _____

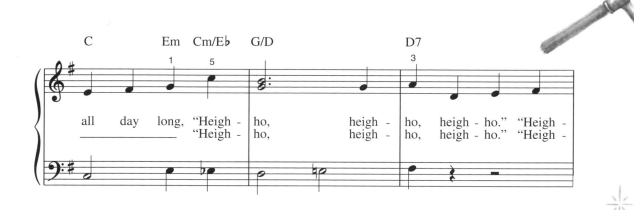

C   Em   Cm/E♭   G/D   D7

all   day   long,   "Heigh - ho,   heigh - ho,   heigh - ho."   "Heigh -
"Heigh - ho,   heigh - ho,   heigh - ho."   "Heigh -

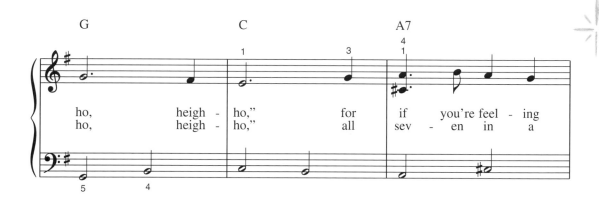

G   C   A7

ho,   heigh - ho,"   for   if   you're feel - ing
ho,   heigh - ho,"   all   sev - en   in   a

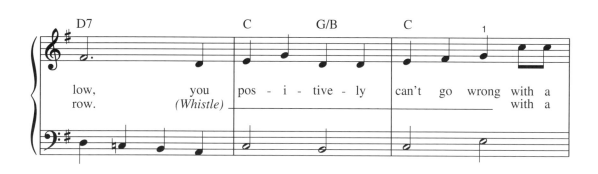

D7   C   G/B   C

low,   you   pos - i - tive - ly   can't   go   wrong   with   a
row.   (Whistle) _____ with   a

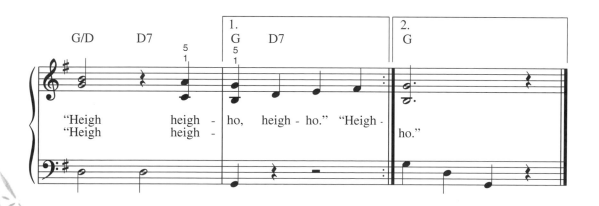

G/D   D7   1. G   D7   2. G

"Heigh   heigh - ho,   heigh - ho."   "Heigh -
"Heigh   heigh -   ho."

I'm Wishing

from Walt Disney's *Snow White and the Seven Dwarfs*

Words by Larry Morey • Music by Frank Churchill

Moderately, freely

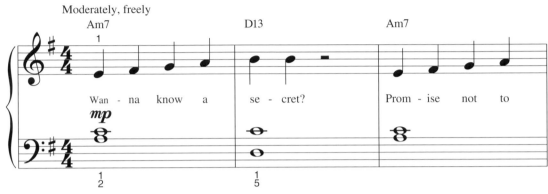

Wan - na know a se - cret? Prom - ise not to

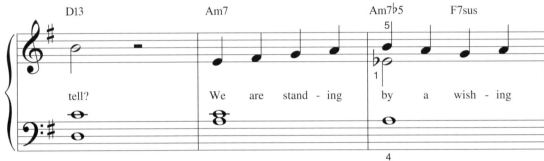

tell? We are stand - ing by a wish - ing

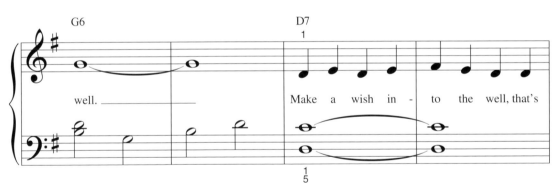

well. _____ Make a wish in - to the well, that's

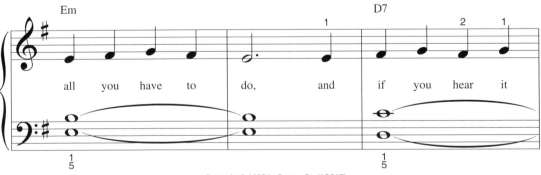

all you have to do, and if you hear it

ech - o - ing, your wish will soon come true. _____ I'm

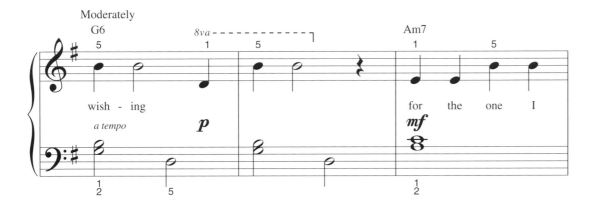

Moderately

G6

wish - ing

Am7

for the one I

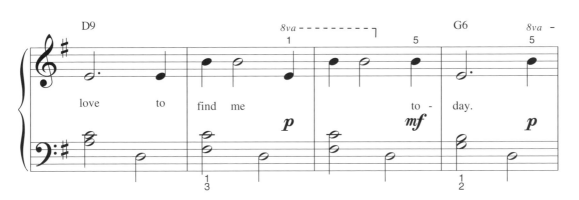

D9

love to find me to - day.

G6

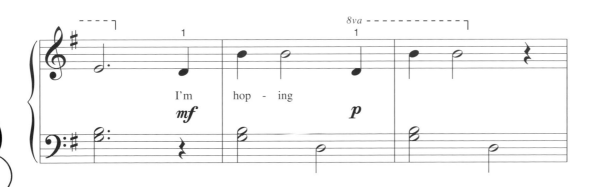

I'm hop - ing

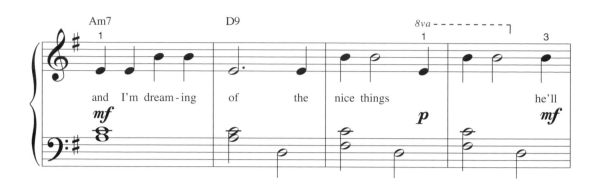

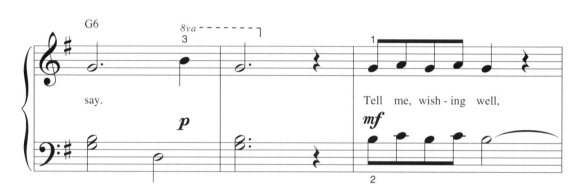

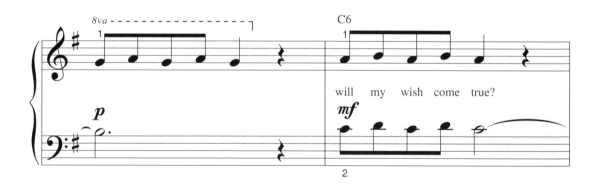

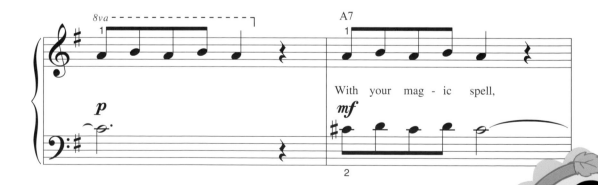

Slower

won't you tell my loved one what to

do? I'm wish - ing

for the one I love to find me

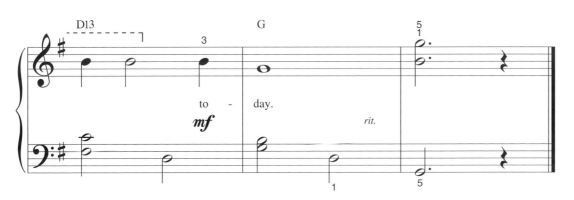

to - day.

Some Day My Prince Will Come

from Walt Disney's *Snow White and the Seven Dwarfs*

Words by Larry Morey • Music by Frank Churchill

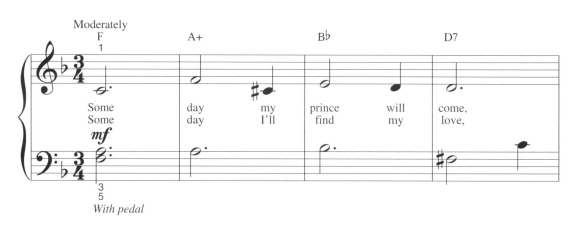

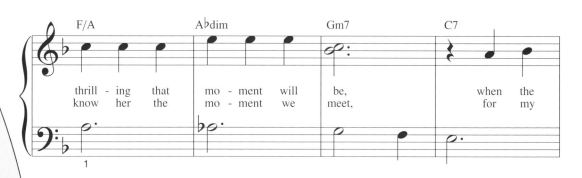

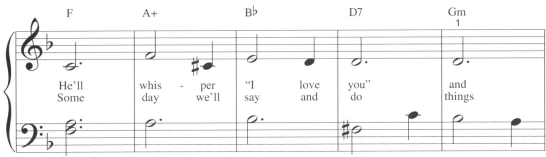

F　　　　　A+　　　　　B♭　　　　　D7　　　　　Gm

He'll whis - per "I love you" and
Some day we'll say and do things

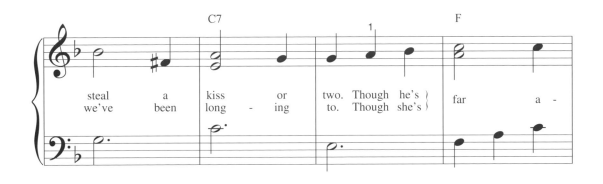

C7　　　　　　　　　　　　F

steal a kiss or two. Though he's far a -
we've been long - ing to. Though she's

A7　　　　　B♭　　　　　Bdim　　　　　F/C

way I'll find my love some day, some day when my

2　　　　1　　　　　4

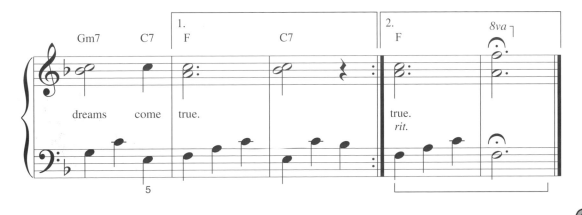

Gm7　C7　　1. F　　　　　C7　　　　2. F　　　　8va

dreams come true.　　　　　　　true.
　　　　　　　　　　　　　　　　rit.

5

53

Whistle While You Work

from Walt Disney's *Snow White and the Seven Dwarfs*

Words by Larry Morey • Music by Frank Churchill

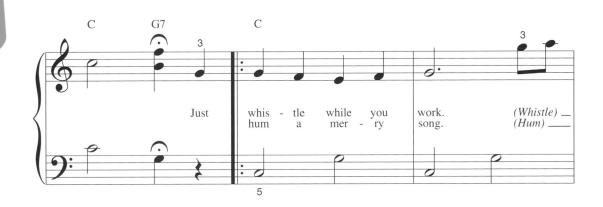

Just whis - tle while you work. (Whistle) __
hum a mer - ry song. (Hum) __

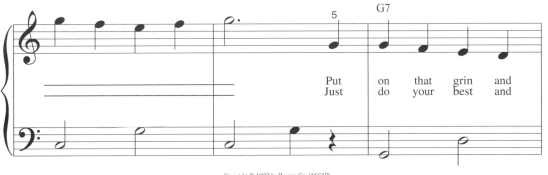

Put on that grin and
Just do your best and

start right in to / whis - tle loud and / long. Just
take a rest and / sing your - self a

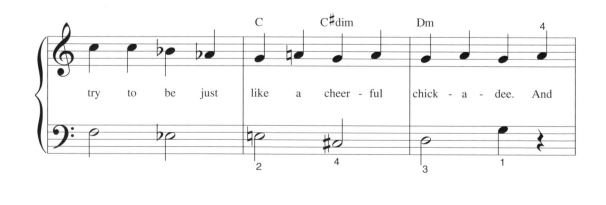

song. When / there's too much to / do, don't

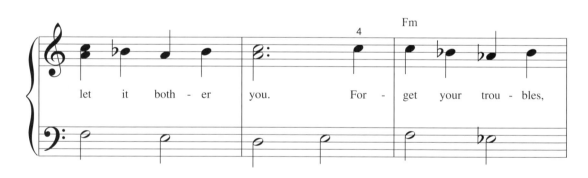

let it both – er / you. For - get your trou - bles,

try to be just / like a cheer - ful / chick - a - dee. And

whis - tle   while   you   work.   *(Whistle)* _____

_____ |_____   Come

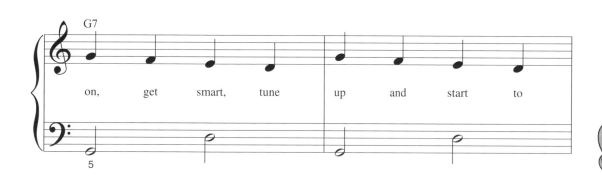

on,   get   smart,   tune   up   and   start   to

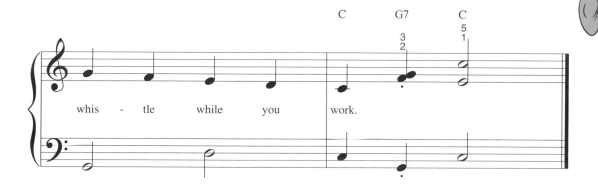

whis - tle   while   you   work.

Who's Afraid of the Big Bad Wolf?

from Walt Disney's *Three Little Pigs*

Words and Music by Frank Churchill • Additional Lyric by Ann Ronell

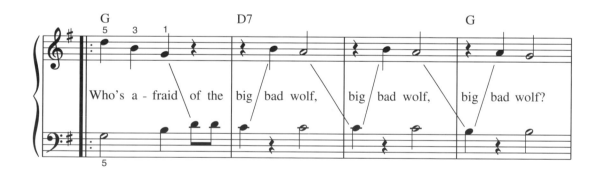

Who's a-fraid of the big bad wolf, big bad wolf, big bad wolf?

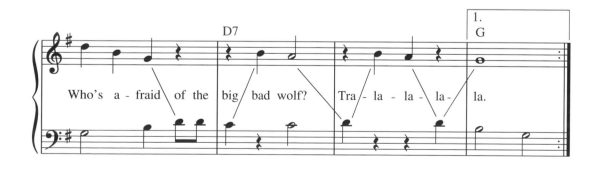

Who's a-fraid of the big bad wolf? Tra-la-la-la-la.

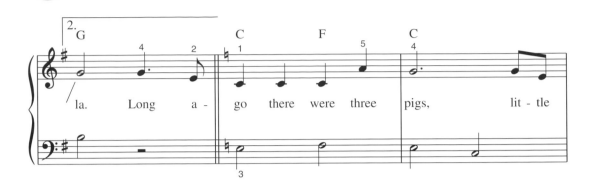

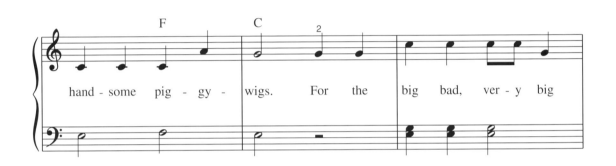

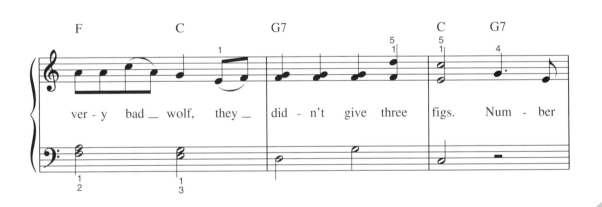

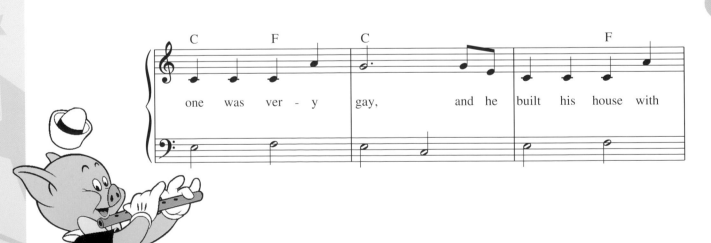

hay; with a hey hey toot, he blew on his flute and he

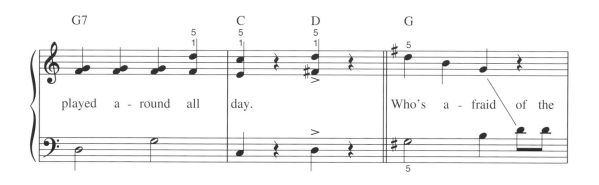

played a - round all day. Who's a - fraid of the

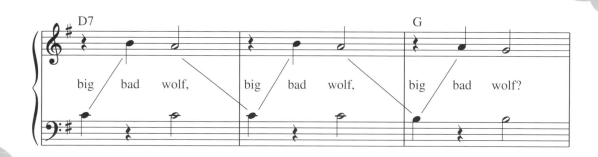

big bad wolf, big bad wolf, big bad wolf?

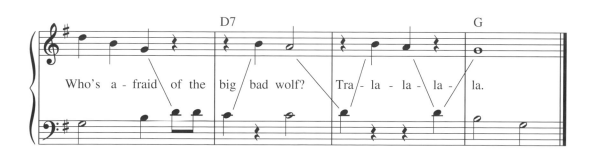

Who's a - fraid of the big bad wolf? Tra - la - la - la - la.